BIBLE VISUALS international

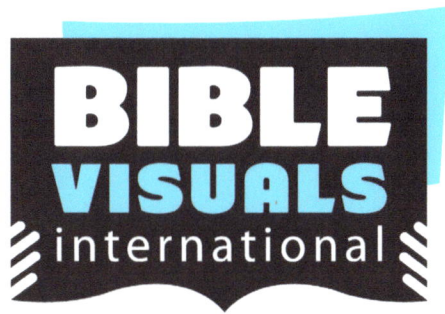

Helping Children See Jesus

ISBN: 978-1-64104-129-4

Be The One
The Todd Beamer Story

An adaptation of Let's Roll! by Lisa Beamer and Todd Anderson
Adapted by Elaine Huber and Judy Bowles
Artists: Scott Gladfelter, Linda McInturff, Jonathan Ober, and Yuko Kishimoto
Page Layout: Patricia Pope

© 2020 Bible Visuals International
PO Box 153, Akron, PA 17501-0153
Phone: (717) 859-1131
www.biblevisuals.org

RELATED ITEMS

To access related items (such as activities, memory verse posters and translated texts) please visit our web store at shop.biblevisuals.org and enter 5010 in the search box on the page.

FREE TEXT DOWNLOAD

To access a FREE printable copy of the teaching text (PDF format) in English or other available languages, enter S5010DL in the search box. Add the item to your cart, and use coupon code XTACSV17 at checkout. Once your order is processed you will receive an email with a link to the free download.

Be the One!

"I can do all things through Christ..."

Philippians 4:13a

Show Illustration #1

In just a few days it would be Christmas 2001, but Lisa didn't feel like celebrating. *Very slowly* she set a box of decorations on the coffee table. Three-and-a-half-year-old David waited impatiently. His Christmas stocking was in that box! And he wanted that stocking hung on the mantle so it could soon be stuffed with Christmas goodies.

Three months before, a very evil plot had disrupted more than their little Beamer family. Terrorists had taken over four different U.S.

airline flights and crashed them, first into New York's Twin Towers, then into the Pentagon in Washington, and into a deserted field in western Pennsylvania. By the end of the day over 2,800 people had died.

During that terrible Tuesday in September, known as 9/11 (nine eleven), ordinary people had suddenly become heroes–Lisa's husband, Todd, among them. Todd had been no more "special" than the others who had tried to turn back the terrorists and keep things from becoming worse.

Lisa was proud of what her husband had done. Perhaps it would be easier to celebrate Christmas if she again thought through why Todd had been so *ready* to be useful to God.

Chapter 1

BE THE ONE: Seek God's *Know How*–Do the Right Thing

Show Illustration #2

As a youngster, Todd had a creative, busy mind. He concocted ways to make happen what he liked and change what he didn't–such as going to bed on time.

One bedtime, Todd put away his toys, put on his pajamas, and even brushed his teeth. But when he knelt beside his bed to pray, he stalled.

"Thank you, God, for my bed . . . and curtains . . . and carpet . . . and bathtub . . . and walls, and . . ."

When Mom opened her eyes and saw Todd scanning the room for more ideas, she stopped him from praying around the whole house.

Show Illustration #3a

Todd was smart enough to stop trying to fool Mom during bedtime prayers. But he didn't lose his respect for prayer. His family had taught Todd that God loved him and cared about Todd's every need. So when he and five-year-old Keith Simpson couldn't find the frog they'd been playing with, they agreed: "At supper tonight, let's ask God to help us."

No sooner had Todd arrived home than Mrs. Simpson called Todd's mom.

"Tell Todd that Keith couldn't wait till supper; so right after Todd left, he went to his room to pray. Then he went out back . . . and there was the frog!"

For Todd, that answer to prayer was as big a *miracle* as Jesus healing a blind man or raising Lazarus.

But even if Todd appreciated God's help with some problems, he decided to take care of others by himself–like piano practice. One day, he got so bored with the same old routine that he lay down on the floor, lifted and lowered first one foot and then the other, and slowly picked out each note of the annoying song with his toes!

In a nearby room, Mom heard a strange new touch. She came over to look.

"Todd," she sighed. "Whatever are you up to?"

Todd did have a serious, intense side though. Sports brought that out. As a nine-year-old, he joined Little League and for a while enjoyed switching between playing shortstop, center field, and pitcher. But one day when he was 12, during a very tight game, pitching suddenly was less fun.

"Todd!" the manager signaled. "Hustle out . . . take the pitcher's place."

Me? Todd worried, running onto the field. *It's the last inning . . . bases are loaded . . . two outs.*

Out on the pitcher's mound, he felt pressured to perform. *I gotta strike that guy . . .* **out!**

Todd wanted desperately to save that game for the team. *I'll give it everything . . . Don't know though . . .*

He wound up and sent the ball flying toward the batter. Okay that time. But another of his pitches strayed, walked the batter, and forced in the winning run. His team lost.

Todd slouched off the field, hurt and half angry. But he soon felt his dad's arm around his shoulders.

"You were in a tough spot out there, son."

Sure was, Todd nodded.

"If you're *never* in a tough situation, it's probably because nobody believes you can handle it."

"That's what worried me," Todd sighed.

"Your coach believed in you, Todd. He trusted you to do your best, and you did. That's all anybody can ask."

Surprisingly, Todd wasn't bothered by things beyond his control–at least not on his first plane trip.

Show Illustration #3b

The year Todd was in seventh grade, he and his youngest sister Michelle flew from Illinois to Ohio to visit their grand-parents. On the way to the airport Todd felt the bitter cold and saw the ice building up on the roads. But since Todd had no idea that such weather could cause a very bumpy flight, he fell asleep as soon as he settled into his assigned seat.

Takeoff went fine. But soon the plane began pitching and bumping from one pocket of bad weather to another. Michelle panicked and grabbed the armrests. She looked over at Todd who was sound asleep.

Urrrrr! She groaned.

In time, the jet descended for a stopover. But the runway was so icy that the plane began to skid. Passengers screamed hysterically as the jet slid . . . right off the runway. Almost beside herself with fright, Michelle glanced in Todd's direction.

Still sound asleep.

Frustrated, she let go of the armrest, picked up a pencil, and jabbed him awake.

Show Illustration #4

Past the fright, neither Michelle nor Todd thought much about the incident. All Todd knew was that *sometimes a guy could make good things happen and sometimes he couldn't. If he couldn't, what good did it do to get all worked up?* He'd learned to think like that from those breakfast-time Bible readings of Proverbs. The Beamer kids were learning godly wisdom to help them wisely handle any situation they'd face. Godly wisdom was really taking shape in Todd's heart.

The summer before his eighth grade year, as Todd and his junior high basketball coach shot hoops together, he heard a lot of other good advice.

"Play for the Lord, Todd. . . . Play for success. . . . Don't get down on yourself when things aren't going well. You're too good a player to let that happen."

Todd got to test that advice during soccer. He and an opponent raced from opposite directions. *Whack*–the opponent's head missed the ball and connected with Todd's head.

Determined not to lose a second of action, Todd reached into his mouth, yanked down the two front teeth that had been shoved up into his jaw, and charged on. But when the play was suspended, he discovered that the jaw was no longer in one piece.

As the doctor wired it shut, Todd realized that he wouldn't be talking for a while and that he would be *drinking* his food. But he was determined to make his words understood and not lose weight. After six weeks of liquefied potatoes, meat, gravy, lasagna–even pizza–he hadn't lost a single pound.

At Wheaton Christian High School, Todd was teased about lugging home every book in his locker. But studying hard got him into college in California. After a change in his studies, he transferred to Wheaton, a Christian college in his home state of Illinois. There Todd added sports, fun and friends to his intense study.

Show Illustration #5

Sports earned Todd the nickname of "Gamer," the guy who wouldn't let anyone or anything turn him from a goal. During a spring college break baseball game in Florida, Todd came up to bat. The score was 3 to 2 against Wheaton, with bases loaded and two outs in the last inning.

Todd worked the pitcher for a full count–three balls and two strikes. The stands were tense. So was Todd. His parents were watching too.

The pitcher wound up and let go of his best ball. Todd swung evenly and with his full strength . . . and smacked that ball . . . clear out of the park!

Yet, somehow, Todd never thought to brag about himself. He figured admiration was for professional athletes, like the guys on the Chicago Bulls basketball team or the Chicago Cubs baseball team. He was proud that his baseball jersey sported a number 23 just like the jersey of the Bulls' leading man.

But if Todd didn't brag about his sports accomplishments, he also didn't let on who was behind his college pranks. That's because they were reserved for his best friends in the next dorm room.

One day Todd peered down the hallway. *Nobody was coming.* He pushed open the door to Stan and John's room and called out, "Anyone home?"

No one answered. So Todd slipped inside, set an empty sardine can on the heater, cranked up the thermostat, and hurried back to his room. As the hours ticked off, the sickening smell of hot fish oil totally filled Stan and John's room, saturating blankets, clothes–*everything!*

But even though he was a prankster, Todd was fiercely loyal to his friends: Brian, Keith, Stan, and John. The group stuck together like Velcro®.

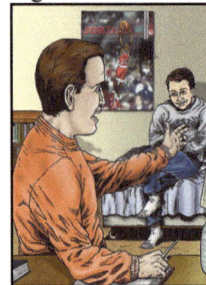

Show Illustration #6

So it was surprising–*or was it?*–that one afternoon during his junior year, Todd exploded into Keith's room and blurted out, "Hey, Franz, I met the woman I'm gonna marry!"

"Good joke. What's her name?" Keith teased.

"Paul Brosius's sister, Lisa. Paul's on my baseball team and Lisa's in a Senior Seminar with me."

"Isn't she practically engaged to some other guy?" Keith quizzed.

"Don't say that," Todd moaned, grabbing his stomach in mock pain and flopping across the bed. "Don't tell me she's taken. She can't be; she's just *perfect!*"

Across campus, not knowing about Todd's interest in her, Lisa Brosius wasn't sure what to think about him. She had spent an entire session of Senior Seminar just watching. *He's a good athlete, captain of my brother's baseball team, and he's not stuck on himself.*

Several weeks later, Lisa asked her roommate, "Kara, have you ever changed your mind about a person when you finally met them?"

"Who?" Kara asked curiously.

"Todd Beamer."

"Oh, him?" Kara added, "Hey, he's a good guy. I'm a trainer for his teams, you know."

"Well, thanks," said Lisa.

Why should you care about Todd Beamer? Lisa scolded herself. *You're dating someone else.* But a year and a half later, at the advice of her mom and a pastor friend, Lisa broke her engagement to the "other" guy. That fall, after graduation from Wheaton, she took a job in Chicago.

Several months later, a friend asked Todd, "Remember Lisa Brosius?"

"How could I forget Lisa Brosius?" Todd smiled. "What about her?"

"Lisa broke her engagement."

"Are you serious?" Todd said, his eyes widening.

"Yep."

"You ought to ask her out, Todd," another friend urged.

Show Illustration #7

The Saturday night Todd took Lisa on their first date, they had to lean into a mean Chicago wind as they walked toward the restaurant.

To be heard above the howl of the wind, Todd cupped his hand and shouted toward Lisa, "This place is famous, but I'm not exactly sure where it is." When they finally found the restaurant, the place was so full that they had to wait and wait.

Lisa worried. *First date . . . long wait . . . probably awkward conversation.*

However, two hours later, when a waiter finally showed them to a table, Lisa and Todd were still talking and enjoying each other's company.

This guy could be a keeper, Lisa thought. *He's motivated . . . intelligent . . . fun to be with . . . great sense of humor.*

But as a Christian, Lisa intended to let God guide her as she carefully chose whose last name she took for life.

Show Illustration #8

In the weeks and months following that first date, whether on the phone or face-to-face, Todd and Lisa learned a lot about each other.

One day, Lisa told Todd, "I was seven years old when I realized I could not do enough good things to please God. I invited Christ to be my Saviour. And like your family, we had daily Bible reading and prayer."

Todd liked what he heard and added, "Christ is my Saviour too, Lisa."

Like opening a storybook and reading it, Lisa began to tell Todd about her childhood.

"I've pulled some stunts, like the time I helped my brother, Paul, give Shep, our German Shepherd, a haircut."

Never one to be outdone, Todd laughed, "Well, one time I got my three-year-old mouth washed out with soap for sassing Mom. And guess who appointed himself as protector of his younger sister? Yup, *me.*"

"Lisa," Todd's eyes grew serious, "we both know Christ. We've both faithfully gone to Sunday school, church and youth group meetings all these years. But I confess, it's time for me to drop my "do-it-my-way" attitude and go for a deeper relationship with God." Lisa nodded in sincere agreement.

"Did you ever play sports?" Todd asked at one point.

Flexing her girlish biceps, Lisa exclaimed, "Did I? I played basketball, soccer and softball. Mom was even my softball coach. And my brother used to brag about his sister flipping baseball cards with the boys and bringing home new cards for his collection."

Like a sports fan Todd cheered for Lisa, "Wow!" and added, "in eighth grade my love for soccer cost me a broken jaw."

Lisa winced sympathetically.

"And in high school basketball," Todd sputtered in mock pride, "to get the slam dunker we needed, I had to dribble right through a guy's legs. Then at Wheaton, baseball earned me the nickname of "No-matter-what guy." In fact, I have the winning baseball on which I scribbled, "Last college hit–solo hit.""

In time, it became obvious that about the only experience that *both* Lisa and Todd had not faced was death. Todd's mom was a stay-at-home mom and his father had a good job with a computer technology company. Lisa's mom was director of a Christian counseling center. But Lisa's dad had died suddenly as a result of a doctor's misdiagnosis when she was 15.

"When the tragedy hit, my world fell apart immediately," Lisa admitted. "I wasn't sure how to go on without Dad. He always made my school friends feel like family . . . hugged and kissed Mom when he got home . . . was always at the supper table . . . and he never raised his voice to get his way."

She knew her dad had loved Christ. She had watched him "walk the talk." Her best memory was that he just knew how to make sense of God and the Bible's difficult-to-understand things. So, when he was no longer there to keep on doing what he always had, Lisa inwardly screamed, "*God, You could have fixed everything if You had wanted to.*"

Lisa's mom consoled her: "For a Christian, this life isn't all there is: Heaven is ahead."

Lisa knew her mom was right. She knew the Bible said at death a Christian is immediately present with the Lord (2 Corinthians 5:5-8; Philippians 3:20; Hebrews 11:10, 16). Still, Lisa could not get over the pain of separation.

Finally, Lisa's church youth leader, Mr. Urbanowicz, helped her think through what it really meant to "let God be God," and her bitterness lessened *just a bit.* Her Sunday school teacher made up for some of the things her father could no longer do. Though Lisa nearly stripped the gears out of his stick shift car, Mr. Daniels taught her to drive. And Mrs. Daniels invited Lisa along on their trip to Wheaton College so that Lisa could make an informed college choice. Once on campus, Lisa knew that after high school, it was Wheaton College for her.

At Wheaton, Lisa signed up for a summer mission trip to Indonesia, *wherever that was.* Going there just sounded like a way to help others and to serve God, that is, until a guy who'd spent the summer there was much too free with stories of bugs, disease and *snakes.*

Wait a minute, Lisa reminded herself. *Why should I worry about what* might *happen? Whatever comes, God will give me the strength to deal with it.*

Show Illustration #9

So, Lisa spent a summer in Southeast Asia, 10,000 miles from her home. She cared for the children of four missionary families who ran a medical clinic. She even weeded their vegetable gardens without seeing a single snake! But, best of all, she taught Bible stories to children and shared her love for Christ to tribal people as the missionaries translated the Bible.

At the end of that summer, though Lisa returned to America less fearful of doing what God wanted, that old anger over her dad's death bubbled up again. So she visited Mr. Massaro, the man who had signed her up for the mission trip. He seemed to understand college students and their frustrations.

Show Illustration #10

Mr. Massaro listened quietly, then responded firmly, "You know, Lisa, God could have changed your dad's hospital or the doctor who treated him. God could have healed your dad. But He allowed it to happen. Maybe it's time for you to accept that."

Lisa was irritated by the sharp words. But since Mr. Massaro didn't give her a chance to talk back, she just listened. And then, strangely, she began to feel herself giving the whole big struggle to God. Lisa figured her change of heart had actually started earlier that week after she had read (and actually *paid attention* to) Romans 11:33-36.

Now Lisa told herself what Mr. Massaro had said: *You don't have God's wisdom or knowledge. You get angry when you don't get the happy life that you think you deserve.* She had finally, consciously chosen to stop questioning God, and was free **not** to be angry about a death she could not reverse. It was just that simple.

Now, with her long battle with God in the past, Lisa was happy that Todd–the guy she was coming to love–had never struggled with death. She hoped he never would.

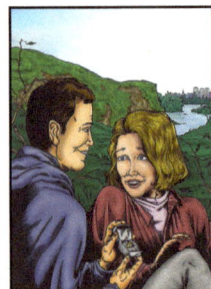

Show Illustration #11

By fall 1993, all Todd could think of was popping the question to the girl who had captured his heart. So, on Thanksgiving Day, at the top of Turkey Mountain, as he and Lisa watched the Hudson River meander toward New York City, he asked innocently, "Well, would it be so bad to be my wife?"

Lisa checked Todd's eyes. Seeing a give-away twinkle, she said, "No, but if this is a proposal, shouldn't I say, 'Yes'?"

"Well, will you marry me then?" Todd asked.

"Yes, Todd," Lisa said happily.

After their beautiful May 1994 wedding, the Beamers settled down into married life in New Jersey. Their greatest desire was to become a godly couple that God could use. Lisa became involved in their church's Bible studies for women, and Todd connected with the youth group.

Todd was a natural with disengaged kids–the ones who were hung up with being a teenager or relating to God. Whether he was shooting hoops with them or driving them somewhere in the church bus, he managed to turn their minds to the Lord Jesus, and they responded with enthusiasm and admiration.

Lisa figured, *If Todd clicks like this with teens, he'll make a super dad.*

And so four years after they were married, Todd was right there with Lisa in the hospital room as she delivered their first child. Excited, Todd hoisted little David into the air, only to have the nurse interrupt with, "*Ahem, Mr. Beamer, it's time for the medical staff to care for your baby.*" Todd leaned close and whispered to Lisa, "I'm going along with the nurse so nobody can switch our baby!"

Show Illustration #12

Todd loved being a dad and was glad that two years later baby Drew joined the Beamer team. As the boys grew, Todd taught them to catch a ball, put on protective sports gear, sack out to watch sports events on TV–even if Todd's favorite team failed to make the playoffs.

Todd's patience with his sons showed God's work in his heart. When David and Drew needed motivating–a push to do what they didn't want to do–Todd got results in a unique way. He just gave a "Todd whistle" or said in a happy, commanding "Todd voice"–*Let's Roll!*–and it always worked.

What was harder for Todd to manage was his work. He was a top salesman for a major software company, and his athletic "go-for-it" style made him work extra hours to succeed. Lisa frequently reminded him, "Todd, please rethink your workload."

Todd really did care about his tendency to overdo, so he prayed about it as he read the Bible. He also asked the men in his Bible study group to help him. Gradually, with God's guidance, his roles became very clear. "I have only one shot at being a good husband and father," he said. "I'd better find out what is most important in life and do it."

Todd did change. He allowed fewer overbusy days, passed up a work promotion, and set his Palm Pilot alarm for 5:30m. Little David would say "Pack it up, Dad!" when he forgot his commitment to his family. Todd switched gears and became a family man.

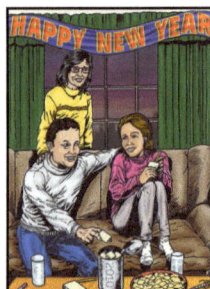

Show Illustration #13

So, on New Year's Eve 2000 a content Todd, Lisa, David, and Drew joined Lisa's family to welcome in the new century. The highlight of the party was making a family time capsule to fill and bury, not to be unearthed until 2010.

Todd directed Lisa, "Here's your paper and pen. We have to write what we expect life to be like in 10, 20 or 30 years."

Todd, the "go-for-it" guy, wrote, "I'd like to be president of my own company, the father of three, and spending more time with Lisa and the kids."

Lisa wrote, "My husband and our two boys will still live in New Jersey, but there will be three children and no more telemarketing calls."

However, as Lisa stuffed her paper into the time capsule, she couldn't shake an unwelcome thought: *What if one of us isn't here in 10 years?*

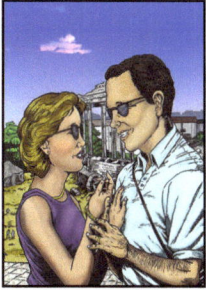

Show Illustration #14

"These company vacations are great," Todd said as he and Lisa strolled hand in hand down a winding, narrow street in faraway Italy. Lisa agreed, "Yes, these trips give us time alone and our parents extra hours to enjoy David and Drew." Lisa's lovely tennis bracelet, purchased for her by Todd during that vacation, sparkled under the Italian sun as they viewed the ancient ruins below them.

But ten days of shopping, sightseeing and enjoying chocolate gelato cones* went by much too quickly. The last evening in Rome, Italy, Lisa and Todd went to bed early in preparation for their scheduled 4:00 a.m. flight to the States the next morning.

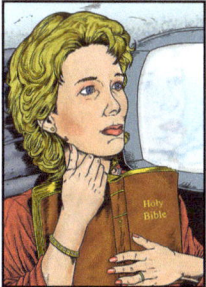

Show Illustration #15

On the long flight home, Lisa saw Todd gearing up for work. She knew what he was thinking: *Long flight home today. Tomorrow morning an early flight to San Francisco. Red-eye flight back same evening. Phew!*

Lisa thought ahead to the women's Bible study she was to teach on the life of Esther. This innocent Jewish girl, unexpectedly crowned Queen of Persia, hadn't even gotten used to being queen before her guardian, Mordecai, had begged her to do the unthinkable: to get the king to block Haman's plans to destroy every Jew in Persia.

Esther had hesitated. Her husband, the king, sometimes killed people who invited themselves into his throne room. But Mordecai had been persistent: "Esther, maybe you are here for a time like this. Decide if you want to *Be the One* God uses to stand in the way of evil."

Lisa figured that choice must have been hard for Esther. But it had allowed her to *Be the One* God used to save a nation.

Lisa's eyes scanned the Bible verses assigned for the lesson, Romans 11:33-36. (*Teacher:* Read these verses aloud to the class from your Bible.)

Suddenly it hit Lisa that these were the verses that had helped her release her anger over her dad's death. Silently she prayed that God's centuries-old truths would do something special for each lady in her Bible class back in New Jersey.

Late afternoon, Monday, September 10, the long flight ended at Newark Airport. Lisa and Todd hurried to meet Lisa's mother and their boys in a parking lot along the highway. By then it was raining so hard that all they could do was dash between cars, shifting luggage and shouting, "How was the trip?" and "It was great."

"Talk later," they promised each other.

At home, Lisa warmed the meal her mom had sent along while Todd hauled the suitcases upstairs. Soon she heard squeals of delight as Dad and sons rolled on the playroom floor and scattered toys all over the place.

After the boys were tucked in bed, Todd made phone calls and downloaded emails. About 9m. Lisa slid under the sheets and drifted toward sleep.

When Todd's alarm jerked Lisa awake, she could feel her body still ticking on Rome time, so she pulled the covers up to keep out the morning light.

If it's Tuesday morning, she half-thought, *Todd's the one who has to get to the airport.*

As she drifted back to sleep, Lisa only partly sensed Todd getting ready, maybe coming back for a good-bye kiss, maybe even saying something. *Whatever. . . .* He'd be back late evening.

Show Illustration #16

Ready to roll, Todd hopped into his car and headed toward the airport. Scattered across the seats lay familiar travel items, plus a pack of Scripture memory cards. The top card in the tray between the bucket seats had the same verses from Romans 11 that Lisa was studying for her Esther class. (*Teacher:* Read aloud Romans 11:33-36 again.)

Even at 6:15 in the morning, it was a beautiful September day, the kind to make a guy want to head outdoors to bat a ball around. But business was business, and today that meant a flight to California.

At the airport, Todd checked himself in and scurried to the gate. He boarded and belted himself into his seat in Row 10. He looked at his watch and talked to himself. *This will be a six-hour flight. Maybe I can get some office work done in that time.*

Although the plane pushed back from the gate at 8:01, there was the usual Newark runway wait–this one, 40 minutes. But takeoff was uneventful and the view was gorgeous.

Approximately five minutes into the flight, as the plane climbed over the New York/New Jersey coastline, a crew member spotted way too much smoke rising from New York City. He called air-traffic control on the ground.

"Everything is fine," was all they knew to tell the Flight 93 crew member.

After another 20 minutes into the flight, things still *seemed* fine. What passengers didn't know as they began eating breakfast was that the cockpit had just been flashed a three-word warning: *Beware–cockpit intrusion.*

"Confirmed," the pilots signaled back to air-traffic control but kept the information to themselves. None of them had any idea that back in Manhattan, United Flight 175 had already been stormed by terrorists and slammed into one of New York City's Twin Towers.

IN THE BEAMER HOME

At the Beamer home, Lisa ignored the phone as she headed out for groceries.

However, as the recorder kicked in, she heard, "Lisa, I was calling to check on Todd. He flies today, doesn't he?"

"Elaine, what's up?" Lisa said, picking up the receiver.

For more information on gelato, which is an Italian ice cream, visit www.slowtrav.com/italy/gelato.htm. Please note that BVI does not necessarily endorse the contents of this web site.

Elaine instructed Lisa, "Turn on your TV. A plane has flown into the World Trade Center."

Show Illustration #17

Lisa grabbed the remote and turned on the TV. What she saw was horrible. But the next news bulletin grabbed her in an even worse way: two planes *were missing*–one from American Airlines, the other from United Airlines.

I don't even know what airline Todd's flying with today, Lisa thought helplessly.

She dialed Continental Airlines, but they wouldn't share passenger information.

Sometimes Todd goes United, she remembered. But all she got when she phoned United was, "All representatives are helping other customers."

Frustrated, Lisa called her friend's number. Elaine's husband answered, "I'll try to track down Todd's flight information, and I promise to send my wife over to stay with you, Lisa."

ABOARD FLIGHT 93

As Todd's flight neared Cleveland's air space, traffic controllers first heard the pilot's cheery "Good morning," then violent noises, scuffling, and repeated commands to *"Get out of here . . ."*

In Row 10, Todd felt the plane begin to bounce up and down *violently*. Then an out-of-breath, heavily-accented voice broke the tense silence:

"Ladies and gentlemen, it's the captain . . . . *Keep remaining sitting."*

Todd didn't think such grammar sounded like an airline captain.

Then the thick voice announced, "We have a bomb . . . *stay sitting."*

Show Illustration #18

Todd didn't stay seated in Row 10 because the guy with the "bomb" strapped around his waist ordered him to Row 27. There Todd sat down next to a flight attendant.

Up in the fourth row, a man spoke softly to his wife on his personal cell phone.

"Honey, it's Tom. We've been hijacked. Somebody's been knifed. There's a bomb on board. Please call the authorities."

As the plane made an abrupt U-turn, Tom added, "They're turning the plane back to New York . . . no . . . *south.*"

Tom figured, from what his wife said, that Flight 93 appeared to be on a suicide mission.

In the cockpit, the injured pilots were lying motionless on the floor and couldn't respond to the government order to land. Out in the cabin, cut off from all communication, none of the passengers knew the President had just announced that America was under a deadly terrorist attack.

A man near Todd, Jeremy, got a call through to his wife. She confirmed that *two* planes had now been flown into the Twin Towers. "Is that where Flight 93 is headed?" Jeremy asked. She didn't think so since both towers had already been destroyed.

The hijackers in the cockpit, now in control of the flight, switched off the plane's automatic controls. Flight 93 began wildly changing speeds . . . plunging . . . lurching . . . bobbing. . .

Todd ignored the hijacker with the "bomb" around his waist, and grabbed the Airfone in the seat in front of him.

Chapter 4
BE THE ONE: Cooperate with God–Show His Great Love

Show Illustration #19

Todd's call from United Flight 93 got through to the GTE desk. Mrs. Jefferson, tipped off that Todd's call was from a flight in trouble, used her training to respond in an assuring manner to Todd. But it wasn't easy to say calmly, "This is Mrs. Jefferson speaking. Sir, I've been informed that your plane is being hijacked. Please give me detailed information."

Todd relayed what the flight attendant next to him knew:

"We think . . . about 27 passengers in the coach section . . . no children . . . ten in first class, five flight attendants . . . *three hijackers . . . two with knives . . . one with a bomb around his waist . . . two people on the floor . . . probably pilot and copilot . . . unsure whether dead or alive."

"Your name, sir?" the operator asked.

"Todd Beamer, from Cranbury, New Jersey."

Up front, Tom got through to his wife again. The news was worse. Now the Pentagon in Washington, DC, had been hit by a plane likely commandeered by more hijackers. Tom told his

* The U.S. Government reported four hijackers. Todd was only stating what he knew at the time.

wife that a group of Flight 93 passengers were talking about doing something to take charge of their flight.

Back in Row 27, Todd listened to Mrs. Jefferson's instructions. If he felt he was risking his life talking to her, he was welcome to put the phone *down* but without hanging up.

Todd said he was not being threatened but wondered whether he should call his wife. Yet when Mrs. Jefferson volunteered to connect them, Todd hesitated. He said he just wanted to let someone know what was going on in case it might help. He thought the flight was heading back to Newark.

Then Todd's voice tightened.

"Now we're going down . . . down . . . back up . . . north. I don't know **where** we're going. **Oh, Lord Jesus, please help us! . . . LISA . . . !"**

"Yes?" Mrs. Jefferson asked.

"That's my wife's name," Todd explained.

"That's my name too," replied Mrs. Jefferson.

As Todd felt the plane again weave wildly, he shouted, **"Mrs. Jefferson . . . Mrs. Jefferson."**

"I'm still here," she assured Todd. "I'll be here as long as you are."

Mrs. Jefferson marveled at Todd's calmness. She feared the flight was commandeered to head into yet another U.S.

landmark so she wasn't surprised when Todd told her that the passengers were planning to do something.

Nearby, Jeremy asked his wife what she thought about their rushing the hijackers. She said to go for it. After all, Jeremy was a judo champ.

In the front of the plane, Tom was listening to his wife's advice, but it was just the opposite. She was a flight attendant who'd been trained to sit tight and "not make waves."

Tom balked. "If they plan to run this plane into the ground," he said, "we're gonna do *something*."

IN THE BEAMER HOME

Show Illustration #17

At home in New Jersey, Lisa could not keep back the tears. Young David asked his mommy what was wrong.

"I just don't know where Daddy is right now," she said.

She dialed Todd's business cell phone but heard only: "You've reached Todd Beamer . . . Please leave a message."

Disappointed, Lisa recorded, "Todd, I don't know where you are and *I need to hear from you.*"

Almost right away her portable phone rang, but when she answered, the line was dead. She looked at the clock–10 a.m.

She took her portable phone to the laundry room. It rang again.

"Hello! Hello!" Lisa screamed into the phone. But nobody answered.

When her friend Elaine arrived, they headed for the TV.

"Where is Todd?" Lisa worried. It was terrible to think of innocent people dying in New York and Washington and not be able to do anything about it.

ABOARD FLIGHT 93

Show Illustration #19

Mrs. Jefferson could hardly believe she and Todd still had an open connection. Few other phones were working.

"Mrs. Jefferson, if I don't make it," Todd asked, "would you please tell my wife and children how much I love them? I have two young boys, David and Andrew, and my wife Lisa is expecting our third child in January."

"I certainly will, Todd," she promised.

Then Mrs. Jefferson heard Todd saying that they had decided to go for the guy with the bomb. Mrs. Jefferson knew things were bad.

"Mrs. Jefferson," Todd asked, "Would you recite the Lord's Prayer with me?" Together they prayed. (*Teacher:* Read aloud Matthew 6:9-13. Encourage your students to say it from memory as you read.)

Who could have missed the impact of Jesus' words as Todd and Lisa Jefferson prayed them back to God: "forgive those who sin against me"?

Then, as Todd began saying aloud Psalm 23, Mrs. Jefferson heard others join in. (*Teacher:* Read aloud Psalm 23. Encourage your students to say it from memory along with you.)

Who could have missed the impact of those words as Todd and others quoted them together? ". . . *Yea, though I walk through*

the valley of the shadow of death, I will fear no evil . . ."

When Todd finished encouraging himself and others with the Bible verses, Mrs. Jefferson heard Todd breathe deeply, turn away from the phone, and say to the others, "Are you ready? Okay. **Let's roll!**"

In the galley, a flight attendant told someone on the other end of her connection that everyone was running to first class. Then she laid down the phone.

Jeremy's wife heard him say the same thing: "They're doing it . . ."

Over her connection, Mrs. Jefferson heard shouting . . . clatter . . . screams . . . then **nothing** . . .

She hung on for 15 more minutes. Finally, fellow workers gently moved Mrs. Jefferson away from the silent phone.

IN THE BEAMER HOME

Show Illustration #20

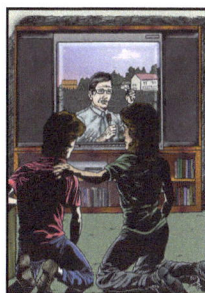

In the Beamer living room, Elaine and Lisa sat stunned as the TV networks suddenly switched to a bare field in Western Pennsylvania. Another plane had crashed.

Todd's plane would have gone in that direction, Lisa thought with a shudder. Cold shivers ran through her body, and a tight knot hit her stomach as she looked at the smoke billowing up from the charred, black ground.

The television reporter broke in with, "The downed plane was a United Airlines flight headed for Chicago."

Lisa figured Todd would have had no time for a Chicago layover. She stood up and nervously inched behind the sofa.

The newscaster corrected his comments, "That was actually a United flight out of Newark to San Francisco."

"No!" Lisa screamed at the television as she dropped to her knees. Elaine ran to Lisa and wrapped her arms around her.

"*Elaine . . . that's **Todd's** plane!"* Lisa cried.

Lisa lumbered upstairs, sat dully on the bed, and stared blankly out the window moaning, "Oh, dear God . . . I **need** Todd. He always made everything okay."

In a short while Elaine's husband appeared with a message from Todd's company. "Todd was booked on that downed flight," he reported. That afternoon, United Airlines called to confirm the same thing. Later, Todd's Wheaton College friend, Keith Franz, telephoned. Overwhelmed by shock and grief, Keith cried as he tried to comfort Lisa.

Now, like Queen Esther of the Bible, Lisa knew she would have to step between evil and those she loved. God and His Word had strengthened her to respond in courage just as Todd had on Flight 93.

The next morning Lisa and David snuggled in the beanbag chair. She held him close as they talked about airplanes and flying like they had done on a family vacation to Orlando, Florida.

Then Lisa said simply, "David, the plane that Daddy was on yesterday had an accident, and . . . and it hit the ground real hard. Everyone was hurt badly . . . and died."

David was only three-and-a-half. He had never known anyone who had died.

"When a person dies," Lisa explained, "he can't come back home, and he can't call us on the phone. . . . But because Daddy loved Jesus, he went to be with God in Heaven . . . and you and

Drew and I will be there with Daddy someday. But today, we're not . . ."

"But Daddy's going to be coming off the plane, right?" David asked.

"No, not this time," Lisa said. "Daddy *wanted* to come back but he couldn't. . . . We won't see him here anymore."

Friday evening the FBI allowed Lisa to read their government report about the hijacking of Flight 93, Todd's flight. They also gave her the telephone number of the last person to speak with Todd. After an emotional and warm conversation with Mrs. Jefferson, Lisa finally understood why Todd had called GTE's Airfone instead of her. He had hoped to pass on vital information to help protect her, their unborn child that she was carrying, the people on Flight 93, and the nation.

That was so *Todd*–accepting the consequences of trying to make a good thing happen. That *Be the One* attitude–Todd's quick thinking, creativity, and deep faith in the Lord Jesus– helped him during the most difficult test of his life.

Show Illustration #21

No wonder in his September 20, 2001, address to the nation, President George W. Bush publicly honored Lisa's response to the tragedy. No wonder the president tucked Todd Beamer's *Let's Roll!* into his State of the Union Address as a symbol of patriotism, faith, and motivation.

Clearly, Todd Beamer was eager to be useful to God. So Todd was honored. His actions, and those of others on Flight 93, cut short the evil plans of the terrorists on that terrible Tuesday, 9/11.

Maybe that's why we still have a White House . . . and a United States Capitol . . . and a president.

It's not easy to *Be the One* God can honor with a hard job. But it's worth the preparation.

* *

Show Illustration #1

Three months after one of America's darkest days, Lisa Beamer *very slowly* set a box of Christmas decorations on the coffee table. Her son, David, immediately pictured his big Christmas stocking hanging from the fireplace mantle.

"Come on, Mom," he exploded. *"Let's roll!"*

Lisa froze momentarily, her mind racing between September 11th and December 25th. *Let's Roll!* had always moved their family to happy action.

She smiled at David and said cheerily, "You're right, David. *Let's roll!*"

Both of them tore into the Christmas decorations.

The Lord's Prayer

Matthew 6:9a-13 KJV

Our Father which art in Heaven,

verse 9a

Hallowed be Thy name.

verse 9b

Yeshua

Jehovah

Jehovah Rapha

Thy Kingdom come. Thy will be done

verse 10a

in earth, as it is in Heaven.

verse 10b

- 32 -

Give us this day our daily bread.

verse 11

And forgive us our debts, as we forgive our debtors.

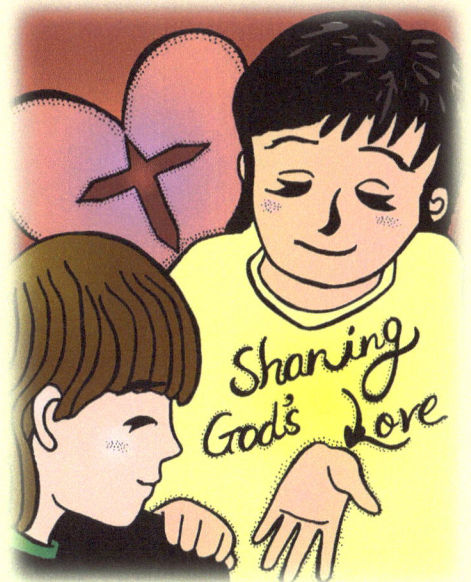

Sharing God's Love

verse 12

And lead us not into temptation, but deliver us from evil:

verse 13a, b

For Thine is the kingdom, and the power, and the glory, for ever. Amen.

verse 13c

www.ingramcontent.com/pod-product-compliance
Lightning Source LLC
Chambersburg PA
CBHW042020080426
42735CB00002B/113